☆☆☆☆☆☆☆

TOMMY:

✩✩✩✩✩✩✩✩✩✩✩

The Civil War Childhood of a President

A Biography

By Julia Faye Smith

© 1996 by Julia Faye Smith

Russell House Publications
1403 Russell Street
Bainbridge, GA, 31717
(912) 246-8803

All Rights Reserved

ISBN 0-9634826-8-8

Photos by Jim Smith Photography, Bainbridge, GA

New Hope Press - Sue Riddle Cronkite
108 9th Street
Apalachicola, FL, 32320
(904) 653-9043

A portion of the proceeds from the sale of this book will be donated to the restoration fund for the Boyhood Home of President Woodrow Wilson. Restoration is a project of Historic Augusta, Inc.

Dedication

To the teachers at Jemison Elementary who long ago gave me
complete access to our tiny school library.
To the teachers at Tuscaloosa Junior and Senior High
who insisted that I learn to write,
To my parents who gave me the belief that I could
accomplish anything,
To Dane, Tricia, and Marc for giving me a reason to try,
and especially,
To Jim, whose faith in me and this project brought it to be,
and for
Leah.

Contents

Prologue   VII

Part 1: The War

Chapter 1 / There'll Be War
News of Abraham Lincoln's election   3
Chapter 2 / The Manse
Moving into the new home in Augusta   7
Chapter 3 / Marching to War
Military parades   13
Chapter 4 / Indians in the Parlor
Learning about power   17
Chapter 5 / Big Steve
Arrival of the fire bell   23
Chapter 6 / All For a Good Cause
Melting a neighbor's fence for ammunition   27
Chapter 7 / Praise the Lord, Pass the Ammunition
Helping the Southern cause   31
Chapter 8 / A Decision is Made
The war brings changes   34
Chapter 9 / The Dead, The Dying, The Enemy
Confederate wounded and Yankee soldiers   39
Chapter 10 / A Place of Peace
Father's church as hospital and prison yard   43
Chapter 11 / Father's Study
Concerns about the Yankee prisoners   47
Chapter 12 / Cowpea Soup and Plug Tobacco
War shortages   53
Chapter 13 / Waiting for Sherman
Anxiety in the face of the enemy   57
Chapter 14 / 'Tis the Season to be Jolly'
How to celebrate   61
Chapter 15 / It's Over
The end of the war   63

Part II: Reconstruction and Beyond

Chapter 16 / The May Day Riots
Life after the war   67
Chapter 17 / A Fallen Leader
Watching Jefferson Davis on his way to prison   73
Chapter 18 / Converting Yankees into Presbyterians
Union soldiers back at the Arsenal   77
Chapter 19 / The Family Grows
Arrival of little brother   81
Chapter 20 / Childhood Friends
Shooting a cousin and controlling friends   83
Chapter 21 / The Reluctant Scholar
Formal schooling   87
Chapter 22 / The Hero
Meeting General Robert E. Lee   91
Chapter 23 / Leaving Augusta
Saying goodbye   97
Epilogue   *101*

Prologue

The future President of the United States stood on the edge of the field fascinated by the parade passing in front of him. He had seen many parades since the war started two years ago, but this one was different. There were no brass bands playing, no freshly uniformed infantry units stepping high, and no prancing cavalry horses. No one was marching, and no one was cheering.

This was not a parade of clean, smartly dressed military men. This was a parade of ragged men in tattered uniforms. Their sabers and sashes were replaced by blood and bandages. And dirt.

There was no one to watch this parade by the railroad tracks in Augusta, Georgia, but seven-year-old Tommy and his young friends. Playing in the fields near the tracks, they had heard the solemn ringing of the troop-train's bell and watched as it shuddered to a stop beside the field. Curious, the boys ran to the train, and watched as slowly it emptied its cargo of Civil War wounded.

A few of the injured limped unaided, but many more shuffled, supported on one or both sides by others who were themselves wounded. Others hobbled on crutches. One man, with a foot missing, kept his head down and his eyes on the bandage at the end of his leg. He seemed to be looking at the foot that wasn't there.

After the walking wounded, came men on litters. Their bodies, their heads, their limbs wrapped in bloody, dirty bandages. Some of the blood was old and caked; some new and oozing.

One man alone seemed to see the boys. His large body was covered with a blood-soaked blanket on which *several medals and many flies competed for space. His head and face were covered with bloody, dirty bandages. One eye was left uncovered. The eye stared at the boys, then down at the blanket-covered body. Finally, it lifted back to the boys, and as the litter moved past them, it swung sideways in its socket to hold them in its view for as long as possible. As the one-eyed, blanket-covered soldier passed, the boys could see that he was crying.*

A foul, wretched smell filled the air though which the litters moved. It was not a smell like the barnyard or cowpen. It was not even a smell like hogs being slaughtered. This smell was worse, much worse. As it grew stronger, Tommy and his friends covered their mouths and noses, as if to protect themselves from this smell which instinctively they knew to be the smell of death.

Finally, from the car nearest the engine came a different sight. Men under guard. Men whose arms and legs were bound together, making it hard for them to walk. So, they, too, shuffled. And they, too, were covered with dirt and blood and bandages.

It seemed unreal, yet as young as the boys were, they knew that it was all too real. The loyal wounded and the enemy prisoners had arrived.

One of Tommy's friends broke their silence. "Come, on," he said. "Lets get back to our game."

Everyone turned to go but Tommy. Tommy stood still, only his head moving to follow the hundreds of wounded and dying soldiers who were passing by.

Finally he turned and headed, not toward his friends, but back to his home and the security of his family. He could play no more that day. He wasn't sure he could ever play that game again.

The boys had been playing war.

✮✮✮✮✮✮✮

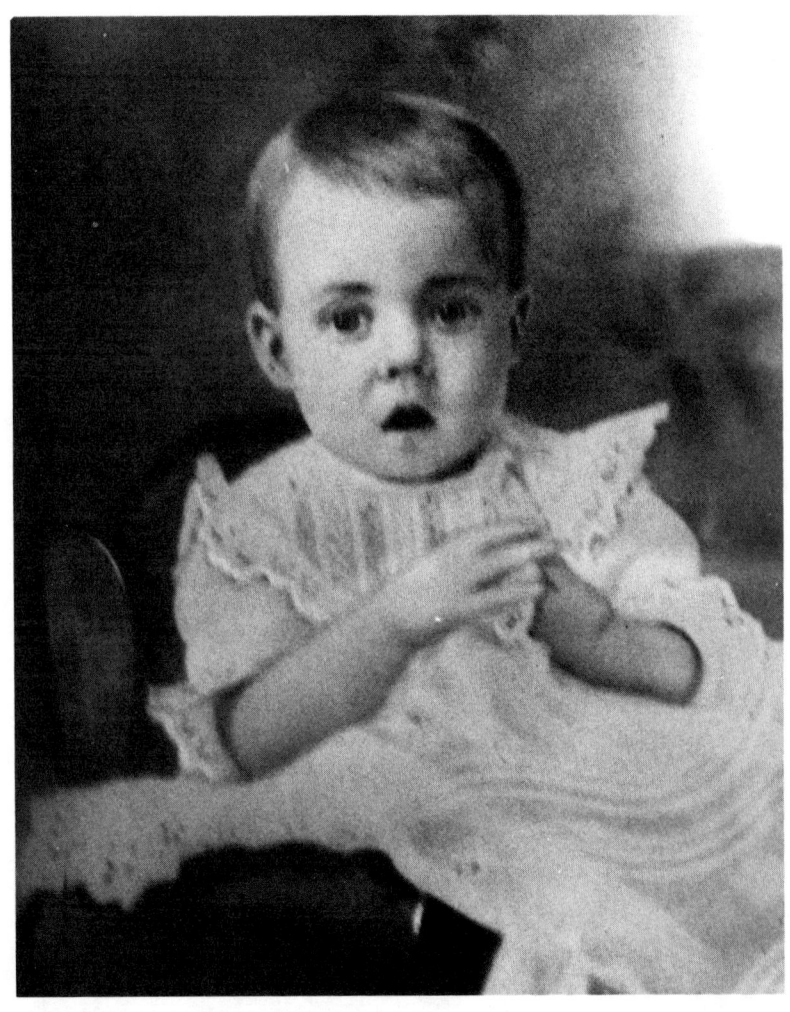

Although no written documentation exists, the descendants of Woodrow Wilson and historical authorities believe this to be a portrait of young Tommy. Permission to use received from Rachel H. Cockrell, director of collections for Historic Columbia Foundation, Columbia, S. C.

Part 1:

THE WAR YEARS

"A boy never gets over his boyhood, and never can change those subtle influences which have become a part of him, that were bred in him when he was a child."
　　　　　　　　　　　　　　　Thomas Woodrow Wilson
　　　　　　　　　　　　　　　　　　October 13, 1904

Chapter I

'There'll be War. There'll be War'

Young Tommy, one month away from his fourth birthday, was swinging on the gate of the fence surrounding his family's home in Augusta, Georgia. Tired of looking through the pickets of the gate, he balanced himself on a cross-bar and stretched to see over the top.

There was great excitement in the street on the other side of the fence. Since early morning, creaky farm wagons, elegant town carriages, and men on horseback had been stirring up clouds of dust as they raced by. Streams of people hurried past on their way to Broad Street just three blocks away.

Tommy wondered what was happening, but knew he could not leave the yard to find out. His older sisters could go outside the fenced yard alone, but he couldn't. On this cool and sunny November day that didn't seem fair, for something exciting was happening.

Suddenly, one man ran back from Broad Street. He was shouting to anyone who would listen. Quickly a crowd surrounded the excited man. At first Tommy couldn't hear the words, but as the man and his audience came nearer, Tommy could hear them clearly.

"Mr. Lincoln's been elected! There'll be war! Mr. Lincoln's been elected! There'll be war."

The people in the crowd began to wave their arms, some shouted and some cried. They all seemed to be talking at once.

The message was repeated over and over. "Mr. Lincoln's been elected! There'll be war!"

Tommy watched for a moment, puzzled by the message and the reaction to it. He didn't understand why the men of Augusta were so excited. What could make some men happy and some sad? He didn't know who Mr. Lincoln was. He didn't understand the word war.

But even at this young age he was curious, and he knew someone who would understand what was going on and who would explain everything to him. Tommy turned from the confusing scene and ran into the house and across the broad central hallway to his father's study.

"Father, father," he called "what's war?"

As Tommy repeated his question to his father, Rev. Joseph Ruggles Wilson knew that Tommy's question was not just idle curiosity. He knew that election news was expected that day and that if Abraham Lincoln of Illinois was elected President many Southerners vowed to go to war. It was late 1860 and the United States of America was troubled.

Patiently Rev. Wilson tried to answer his young son's questions without frightening or confusing him. How could he explain equality, slavery, and States Rights to the youngster? How could he explain that a relative living in the North might disagree with, and fight against, a relative living in the South. Rev. Wilson did his best to help Tommy understand and ended with the hope that the war would not come.

But it did, of course. The American Civil War which the man in Augusta had foretold upon hearing the news of Abraham Lincoln's election, officially began five months later at 4:30 a.m. on the 12th of April, 1861, when Confederate troops fired on Union troops at Fort Sumter, South Carolina. Tommy was then four years old.

In the four bloody years that followed that early morning beginning, young Tommy learned about war. He watched his hometown prepare to send their finest to battle and then mourn for those who did not return. He watched and waited with his fellow citizens when the army of the enemy was on its way to their town. He also watched the wounded and the prisoners of war as they arrived at his doorstep.

Through it all he learned. He learned about the glory of fighting for a belief and the anguish of fighting for a lost cause. He learned about the excitement of a stirring parade and the sadness of a somber parade. He learned about pride and passion and prisoners. He also learned about hurting, healing and heroes.

These lessons he took with him as years later he marched into the Presidency and tried unsuccessfully to keep America out of another war. When he could not, he tried, again unsuccessfully, to establish a lasting peace. He wanted a peace which would guarantee that in the future boys and girls would not have to face what he and his friends had faced.

But on that day in 1860 when the young Thomas Woodrow Wilson ran to his father for an explanation of war, he was not thinking of the distant future. He was trying to understand the changes that were just beginning to surround him and his world.

The Manse, Tommy's boyhood home, as it looks today. Renovation and restoration continue.

Chapter 2

The Manse

Sitting on the front steps of his home, Tommy tried to understand what his father had told him about the new President, Mr. Lincoln, and people who did not like what he stood for. Some people, his father had said, felt that their way of life was being threatened. These people were ready to fight for their beliefs, and many of them lived right here in Augusta.

Tommy looked around at his neighborhood and tried to imagine what it would be like if there were people fighting in the street. He could not. He had known nothing but love and affection from everyone he had met in Augusta since he and his family had moved here from Staunton, Va., two years earlier.

That move, in 1858, had taken Tommy away from his first home which had also been a manse, a home provided by the church. Sitting on a sloping Virginia hillside, that house and its porches had given the family a view not only of their own gardens, but also of part of the town of Staunton and of his father's church and the school where he had taught.

Born December 28, 1856, and christened Thomas Woodrow Wilson after his maternal grandfather, Tommy lived his first year and grew into a toddler there. As the newest member of a close-knit family he was well-loved.

His mother, called Jessie by her family, but christened Janet Woodrow, had been born in England. Along with Tommy's grandparents, she had come to America in 1836. She was quiet and reserved with outsiders, but loving and supportive with her family. Soon after Tommy's birth, she wrote to relatives and described Tommy as plump, healthy, and "the most beautiful baby in the world."

Although Tommy's father was himself born in America, his father, Tommy's Grandfather Wilson, had arrived in America in 1807 from County Down in Northern Ireland. From these Irish roots, Tommy's father inherited a vigorous love of life and a love of the spotlight and applause. He had a sense of humor and enjoyed telling stories. He loved God and was willing to go where needed to do God's work. The move from Staunton to Augusta was in response to that work.

The Wilson's first home in Augusta was an older home. It was big, hard to heat, and still using an outdoor privy. It was three blocks from the Presbyterian Church where Rev. Wilson was the new minister.

Two years later, the family had a new home provided for them by the church. It was here that Tommy was sitting on the steps and thinking. He turned and looked back at his new home. As he did so, he remembered clearly the day they had moved in just a month ago.

It had been a warm, sunny day, just perfect for moving. As the Wilson family stood in front of their new home Rev. Wilson looked at Mrs. Wilson and raised his eyebrows in a silent question.

"It's beautiful, Joseph, really beautiful. After that cold drafty house we just left, I can't wait to start enjoying this new home with its modern conveniences," she said.

"Me too," chimed in Annie, Tommy's sister. "Imagine, indoor plumbing!"

"And gas lights in the bedroom. That will be wonderful," added Marion, the older of the two sisters.

"Don't get your hopes up too much. All those wonderful things may not be working yet," Rev. Wilson reminded them.

"But they will soon, won't they father?" asked Marion.

"Eventually," answered Rev. Wilson.

"Soon, I hope, " said Mrs. Wilson as she put her arms around the two girls and started up the steps to the house. "Come, girls," she said heading toward the front door, "we're home."

Rev. Wilson smiled and shifted young Tommy from his left arm to his right. The youngster gave his father another hug and noticing the serious way his father stared at their new home, he turned his attention toward the house as well. He didn't know what his father might be looking for, but he joined in looking for it with great seriousness.

What Tommy and his father saw was a beautiful home made of red brick and trimmed in white. It was two stories high on the front and three stories high on the sides where the gabbled ends of the attic formed an A-line third floor.

Nine tall windows, framed by green shutters, were like eyes looking toward the street in front of the house. Around all sides, on all floors, the windows continued.

These large windows allowed sunlight to flood the house on sunny days. They also gave those inside a clear view of the world outside.

The entrance porch, nothing more than a stoop at that time, seemed dwarfed by the house. Rising above it all, four tall brick chimneys stood as sentinels on guard.

While Tommy and his father looked at the house, the front door suddenly flew open. Marion ran down the front steps with her dark hair flying behind her. She called to her father in an excited voice. "Hurry, Father. I want to show Tommy his room."

"Yes, of course, of course," Rev. Wilson responded, "you take Tommy inside. I'll just stay out here for a while longer."

Marion took young Tommy in her arms. The sandy-haired youngster with the intense eyes gave her a big sloppy kiss and then blew in her eye. While she was reacting to this familiar playfulness, Tommy squirmed out of her arms and hit the ground running.

Marion caught up with him as he reached the front steps. Although he could manage by himself, he found himself half-hugged, half-scooted up the steps by his older sister. Then, taking his hand, she led him into the wide entrance hall.

Halfway down the long hall were the stairs leading to the second floor. At the bottom of the stairs, Marion tried to pick him up and carry him up the stairs, but energetic and independent Tommy shook his head fiercely. He wanted to climb the stairs himself.

When they reached the second floor. Tommy ran straight ahead to a small room.

"No, Tommy, that's not your room."

"What is it?" Tommy asked as he peeked in.

"That's the indoor privy," said Marion with a certain amount of pride in her voice.

"The what?" Tommy's eyes were round with disbelief.

"The privy," Marion responded with a smile.

"In the house?" Tommy almost shouted the question, then looked around with great interest.

"Yes. Come on," she insisted, "I'll explain it to you later. Don't you want to see your own room?"

Tommy nodded his head and slowly dragged his eyes away from the fascinating new room.

He and his sister were standing in the middle of a large hall at the top of the stairs. Four doors, in addition to the privy, or bathroom, door opened onto this hall. A set of stairs rose upward to the third floor. Tommy headed for the stairs.

"No," said Marion. "Thank goodness your room is not on the third floor. We would never be done with going up and down the stairs with you." Taking his hand, she guided him into a room behind their parents' room.

Tommy's room was large and square, and because it was the nursery in the home, it had a connecting door to his parents' room. The furniture from his old room was already in place and his toys were even placed around the room. His rocker was near the fireplace in front of a tall window.

"Look, Tommy," Marion said as she walked over to the window, "you can see Father's church from here."

Young Tommy could barely peek over the window ledge, but when Marion lifted him he could easily see the large Presbyterian Church sitting cater-cornered across from his family's new home. Tommy didn't know it then, but the scenes he could see from that window would change dramatically in the next few years, and what he saw would remain with him forever and touch his future decisions.

Chapter 3

Marching to War

While he watched, Tommy's world went to war. The early days of the war brought pride and great excitement to the people of Augusta. The citizens believed, as did most Southerners, that the war would be short and they would win. Men of all ages were quick to volunteer to serve their side.

Military parades with snappy drumbeats and high stepping soldiers were a common sight. Tommy lived three blocks from Broad Street, the wide street that was the main avenue for parades in Augusta. Every day local military units drilled up and down while townspeople watched and cheered. When these groups left for battle, there was music and ceremonies, and it seemed almost like a party.

One parade that filled everyone with pride was a special parade and drill held by the Clinch Rifles of Augusta. The Clinch Rifles was a crackerjack unit of sharpshooters. Everyone was proud of their skill and everyone was going downtown to watch this parade, including the Wilson family.

For once it was Tommy who was ready and waiting early. He stood waiting eagerly, not in the house as his sisters might have, but at the front gate, looking down the street toward all the noise. His friend, Joe Lamar who lived next door, had already left with his mother and father and brother Phil.

Tommy was in a hurry. "Come on," he called back toward the house hoping someone would hear and hurry. No one did.

Bored with waiting, Tommy began chasing the butterflies which fluttered around his mother's colorful flower garden. He ran and tumbled but stayed near the front door. He wanted to be ready to leave as soon as the family appeared.

"We're going to miss all the fun if you don't hurry," he yelled loudly toward the house. He couldn't imagine why his family was being so slow on this important day.

Finally, Rev. and Mrs. Wilson and the girls, along with the family's servants, Old Mittie and Samuel, came down the steps. Before opening the gate, Rev. Wilson looked at the small group.

"Now, remember," he began.

"We know, Father," said Annie. The most polite of the children, Annie usually would not think of interrupting her father, but like everyone else, she was caught up in the day's excitement. "We know. Stay together, look out for each other, and hold on to Tommy."

"I can hold on to myself," Tommy protested. "Come on, let's go."

Mrs. Wilson bent down to straighten Tommy's clothes which had been mussed while he was chasing the butterflies.

"Now, honey," she said. "You must hold someone's hand at all times."

Tommy frowned and started to protest. His mother held up her hand to indicate that he should be quiet and listen.

"Tommy, be still and pay attention. The crowd today is going to be very big. Everyone has been looking forward to this day. People have even been coming across the river from South Carolina for this parade," she said, as she looked up to her husband for support.

"Your mother is right. I don't want us to get separated from each other. Does everyone understand?" he asked.

"Yes, Father."

"Of course, Father."

"Okay, Father."

He shook his head and linked his arm with Mrs. Wilson's. "Do you think they understand?" he asked.

"Yes, Father," she said, sounding like her children.

"Will they remember?" he continued.

"Of course, Father," she laughed. "At least they'll try."

They stopped walking and looked at each other and laughed. But they didn't stand still for long. The excitement was too much to overlook.

"Now come on," she said. "Let's go see our Clinch Rifles."

Like the Wilsons, everyone was filled with pride as they watched a special parade and drill held by the Clinch Rifles of Augusta. The Company paraded between 3 o'clock and 4 o'clock in the afternoon. They marched up Broad Street to the commons area and there drilled and exhibited their skills for their neighbors. The crowds at that end of the street cheered wildly.

Then the Clinch Rifles turned and marched to Platt's Furniture on the opposite end of Broad Street. There they were presented with a flag which had been designed especially for them by local women. Turning again, the Company then marched back down Broad Street to more wild cheering from its local supporters and snappy beats from its drummer boy. Finally, they stopped and had their picture taken with their new flag, thought by many to be the first flag of the Confederacy.

Chapter 4

Indians in the Parlor

Everything in Tommy's life, however, did not involve the war. When he was five years old, Tommy heard that Indians were coming to his house.

He was sent upstairs to dress and told to meet the family in the parlor and be ready to greet the guests. When Tommy wasn't at the bottom of the stairs on time, his mother sent Marion upstairs to get him.

As Marion entered Tommy's room, the sight on his bed made her stop and stare.

"Tommy," she was finally able to say, "why is your bed covered with chicken feathers . . . dirty chicken feathers?"

A muffled answer came to her from the closet, one of only two closets in the house, and one of the few in town. Most people, including his sisters kept their clothing in a wardrobe, but Tommy's nursery room, along with his parents' room, had a built-in closet.

"Come out of there this minute and tell me what's going on," Marion said. "We're expected downstairs in a few minutes and mother sent me up to be sure you are ready. Come out and let me see."

Tommy didn't appear and Marion could hear him shoving things around in the closet. Throwing the closet door open wider, she peered in and asked, "What are you looking for?"

"My tomahawk," came the reply.

More thrashing and thumping, so loud that Marion was afraid it would be heard downstairs, sent her into the small space. She looked at her little brother who suddenly stopped his searching and bent and picked up a strange object.

Looking at her with tears in his eyes he said, "it's broken."

"Oh, Tommy," Marion exclaimed, leading him out of the closet and into the bedroom, "please tell me what's going on. Why are you holding two sticks tied together and why are you about to cry?"

"That's my tomahawk" came a soft answer and a sob.

"Why are there dirty feathers on your bed, and why aren't you ready for our company?"

Clearly upset with his older sister, who obviously did not understand, Tommy replied, "I'm trying to get dressed. There are dirty chicken feathers on my bed because the clean ones are on my bureau." He pointed to the corner of the room where his dark bureau was covered with chicken feathers, only slightly cleaner than those on the bed.

Marion looked at them and sighed. "Tommy, please explain, and hurry."

Trying hard not to cry Tommy began. "I'm making an Indian headdress, and I wanted to carry my tomahawk." He sniffed back the tears. "But it's broken."

Marion wasn't sure what to do. Should she try to understand the headdress and tomahawk business, or should she quickly get him dressed and downstairs? Tommy looked up at her. She knew he was fighting the tears so she decided that for the moment she should ignore the obvious cause of his despair and hope he would get over it.

"Tommy, we'll talk about all this later. Right now, you've got to wash your hands and face, comb your hair, and put on your Sunday suit. Then we have to go downstairs and meet father's friends."

"That's what I'm trying to do," Tommy wailed.

"With chicken feathers and a homemade tomahawk, Tommy, I don't understand. I really don't."

"Indians are coming to lunch," he said simply.

"What?"

"Indians are coming and I wanted to dress like them."

Tommy," Marion said with exasperation and amusement mixed, "Presbyterian ministers are coming for lunch. In their Sunday suits, which is what you're suppose to wear. Now let's get dressed, "

"Indians are coming."

"Tommy, please."

Tommy's stubbornness kicked in and he wouldn't allow Marion to help him into his suit. Instead, he worked to repair his tomahawk, made several days earlier. He checked his chicken-feather headdress, blowing on it to make it look fluffier. He wished it was better, but chicken feathers were all he and Joe could find in the neighborhood.

Seeing that she was making no progress with Tommy, Marion left the room. Shortly Mother entered.

"Tommy, you need to get dressed," she said calmly.

"My tomahawk is broken, and I'm not sure my headdress will stay on," Tommy told her. Looking up at her he asked, "Can you fix them?"

She sat down in the rocking chair and pulled Tommy to her side. "Honey," she said, "Indians *are* coming for lunch. But they will not be wearing their Indian tribal dress. They are Presbyterian ministers just like your father, and they will be wearing proper Sunday suits just like your father."

"But I thought . . . ," Tommy started.

"Shh, listen to me," his mother continued. "Even if they were in tribal costume, I don't think it would be right for you to try to dress like them. They might think you were making fun of them and be upset."

"Oh, no, mother. You know I wouldn't make fun of them. I like Indians. When Cousin Jessie and I pretend to be Indians and white men, I always want to be the Indian. You know that."

"I know, honey, but they may not understand. They don't know you, so they don't know you wouldn't make fun of them." She gave him a tight hug and continued. "Now quickly get dressed. In your Sunday suit, please, and come downstairs. I just heard your father come in, and that means the men are here."

Tommy looked at the feathers and the tomahawk and back to his mother. "Are you sure?" he asked nodding toward the Indian headdress.

"I'm sure," she said, "now get moving."

After she left the room, Tommy went to the top of the stairs and listened to the noise from downstairs. Big booming voices, much like his father's, drifted up the stairs. Suddenly the excitement was too much. He turned and ran back to his room to get ready.

"Oh, boy," he said aloud. "Indians in the parlor."

There were, indeed, Indians in the parlor of the manse. Presbyterian ministers from throughout the Confederate States of America were meeting in Augusta. Included among these were Indian ministers from the Choctaw and Creek Nations. These were the Indians that Tommy wanted to impress, but as it turned out, the Indians and the other Presbyterian ministers were the ones who left an impression . . . on young Tommy.

The ministerial meeting involved preaching, debating, holding official meetings, and being entertained at luncheons and dinners in private homes. The sermons and meetings were open to the public, and the public often filled Rev. Wilson's church across from Tommy's home.

Tommy himself would go across the street and watch and listen, especially during the meetings. At these, he saw a leader at the pulpit. A man in charge. A man who controlled who spoke and when. Tommy was greatly impressed by this.

Later, when alone with his father, he asked him about the meetings and the man in the pulpit. His father explained the concept of Parliamentary Procedure for controlling meetings. Tommy watched and listened and committed to memory what he was seeing and hearing. He knew that someday he wanted to use what he had learned to be a leader and control meetings.

Line drawing of Big Steve from poster of typical scenes in Augusta during 1880s. Poster published by Augusta Savings and Loan Association.

Chapter 5

Big Steve

"I love the sound of Big Steve, " Tommy said, as his sister Annie rushed him down the front steps of the manse.

"So do I," she replied, "but we can't stop to listen. You know we should already be at church when it stops ringing."

"I want to look at it," Tommy said, pulling on his sister's hand as he turned to look over his shoulder toward the street behind their home.

"Not today, Tommy. We're already late, and you know how father hates it if we come in after services start."

"Yeah, I know."

"Besides, you'll have lots of time to hear and see Big Steve again," Annie reminded Tommy as they ran across the street to the Presbyterian Church.

☆☆☆☆☆☆

Just as the sound of military parades became familiar to Tommy, there was another sound that became equally familiar. That was the tolling of Big Steve, the town's new fire bell. Big Steve had arrived in Augusta on a warm day in May. It was another occasion that called for a parade.

Covered with jingling bells, flowers, garlands, and a flag, the long-awaited bell arrived at the depot in nearby South Carolina. From there it was taken by wagon across the Savannah River and through downtown Augusta to the intersection of Greene and Jackson Streets, only one block behind Tommy's home. The fife and drum corps led the way while local girls danced along the route. People cheered and sang. The four-ton noise maker received a loud and enthusiastic reception. Soon a five-story bell tower was built on the spot, and Big Steve was raised high above the trees and buildings.

Through the years Big Steve announced many events and became a part of the daily lives of the people of Augusta. From his home close by, Tommy could clearly hear the bell and know that something important was happening in their lives.

When South Carolina became the first state to secede or withdraw from the Union on December 20, 1860, Big Steve tolled one hundred long notes. When Georgia seceded in January 1861, Big Steve again rang the news.

Early in the war the big bell rang twice weekly to call everyone to city-wide prayer meetings. Later in the war, the bell was rung every day at noon to remind the citizens of Augusta to stop what they were doing and pray for the Confederacy.

Tommy's parents joined their fellow citizens in these daily prayers for they fully supported the Southern cause. They saw the war not as a battle over slavery, but a result of the Federal Government and northern states trying to impose their will and conscience on the people of the South. While they did not wish to see the Union broken apart, neither did they wish to see one section of the country crush the will of another.

And so the Wilsons and the South prayed. At first things went well, but as the years passed and the war progressed, it must have seemed to them that God, for whatever reason, was not answering their prayers as they had hoped.

And in the park-like setting surrounding the bell tower, local boys would lie on their backs and discuss the war. As they grew older, Tommy and his friends were among those who felt right at home in the shade of Big Steve.

Chapter 6

All for a Good Cause

As the years passed and the war progressed, it became part of Tommy's life in ways other than watching parades and listening to Big Steve toll the news. Everyday life changed for the people of Augusta. One day Tommy and his friends watched as the war cost their neighbors their decorative iron fence.

"It's all for a good cause," Tommy said, watching workmen remove the iron rails and posts of a fence surrounding their neighbors' home.

"What?" asked Phil.

"It's all for a good cause," repeated Tommy.

"Just what does that mean?" a puzzled Joe asked Tommy. He and Phil had come over bright and early and were sitting with Tommy on the front steps of the Wilson home. Marion and Annie were watching the demolition of the fence from the coolness of the shade under a tree in the side yard of the house. Occasionally the boys turned to wave to them and Tommy's sisters made funny faces in return.

"It means that it's okay to do it," said Tommy.

Joe looked at Tommy, trying hard to understand. "You mean, anything I want to do, even if someone doesn't want me to, I can do if I say it's for a good cause?"

"Yes. Or at least, I think so," Tommy replied. "Mommy said that it was a shame to tear down such a beautiful fence, but Father said he understood why it had to be done."

"And did he say it's for a good cause?" asked Joe.

"He said, 'it's for a good cause, Jessie,'" Tommy replied in his best imitation of his father. Joe and Phil laughed hard and rolled around as much as the small stoop would allow.

Tommy's imitations of his father always sent his friends into peals of laughter because his voice was so high-pitched and his father had a deep booming voice. Tommy trying to sound like his father was pure comedy. He knew it, and so did his father. They both enjoyed the humor of it.

After their laughter subsided, Phil looked at Tommy and asked, "what kind of bullets do you think will be made from the fence?"

Phil was the youngest of the three boys, and he knew that Tommy had recently toured the Confederate Powder Works with his father. It was one of the Reverend's learning lessons that he often shared with Tommy. This was one that the other boys envied, for they all wanted to see how the bullets, minie balls, grenades, and other forms of ammunition were made at the works on the Augusta Canal.

"Well, I don't know," said Tommy, then remembering that he had a willing audience, he added, "but I do know, it's for a good cause."

The good cause was the Confederate States of America. The iron rails and posts of the neighbors' fence, along with anything else made of iron, were to be melted down and made into ammunition for the troops.

Tommy and his friends were very interested in the melting down and remaking of the materials into ammunition. It was done at the Confederate Powder Works, located less than two miles from Tommy's home. The Powder Works also made grenades, gunpowder canisters, three-inch rifled percussion shells, cartridges, and minie balls from scratch. After a couple of years of war, the boys knew the importance of these items.

Another local wartime industry of interest to the boys, was the Confederate States Pistol Factory. The Pistol Factory made nearly 2,500 iron-frame Colt repeaters with a 12-stop cylinder between 1864-65.

In addition to ammunition, Augusta supplied thread, cloth, uniforms, and shoes for the Confederate troops. Buckles, buckets, and baked goods were made in Augusta. Late in the war, artificial ice was being made in Augusta in the first such factory in this country. Most of the ice was used in the Confederate hospitals.

These many war-related industries provided a constant reminder that war was near, but they also provided something else. They became new and different "walking classrooms" for Tommy and his father.

Rev. Wilson took Tommy everywhere around town. Tommy was welcome, not only because he was "the Reverend Doctor's son," but also because the people of the town knew that Rev. Wilson was teaching his son about all parts of life.

Tommy and his father visited cotton fields and plantations. They also visited shops, mills, gins, warehouses, factories, furnaces, and farms. The reason for the visits was to increase Tommy's understanding of the world. He learned about planting, growing, harvesting, and ginning cotton. He learned about producing, packaging, and transporting goods.

Back at home Rev. Wilson would discuss the day's visits and have Tommy repeat what he had seen and learned. Anything not understood was discussed fully. Later, after Tommy's formal schooling began and he had learned to read and write, he was required to write about the things he had seen. His father would carefully go over the paper, questioning Tommy when his ideas were not clearly stated. His father would have him write it again and tell him to "say what you mean."

Then Tommy would be asked to present his ideas orally. Again Rev. Wilson was observant and demanding. "Shoot your words straight at the target. Don't mumble and fumble." he said.

While these trips gave Rev. Wilson the opportunity to teach Tommy practical lessons, they also gave him the opportunity to help shape his son's character. Not only did they see the factories and warehouses around town, but they also saw the people in charge of these places and how they treated their workers. Fairness and equality or unfairness and inequality were more easily understood by Tommy in these on-the-spot classrooms than they might have been through lectures.

His "walking classroom" trips with his afather were frequent and welcomed by Tommy. They would provide some of his favorite childhood memories and he would later call his father the best teacher he ever had.

Chapter 7

'Praise the Lord and Pass the Ammunition'

One Sunday morning Tommy sat in the family pew with his mother and sisters. He was at home not only in the pew but throughout the massive church. Usually he was able to sit still while waiting for his father to enter the large wooden pulpit which was located slightly to the right of the center of the church, but today the warm May weather and his Sunday clothing made Tommy unusually uncomfortable.

As he waited for his father he counted again the sets of windows in the church. "Four, five, six," he turned to the left side.

"Tommy, be still," his mother whispered.

Tommy didn't have to turn, he knew that there were six sets of windows on the left wall to match the six sets on the right wall. Glancing back to the windows that he could see without turning, he tried to estimate their height by closing one eye and trying to decide how tall one foot would be.

"Ten feet, twenty feet, thirty feet, well, maybe too much. Twenty feet, maybe twenty-five feet high," he muttered to himself. "Father wants me to be exact, but he will never let me climb up and measure those windows."

Sighing, Tommy looked up at his father who now stood looking out over his congregation. Even from the family pew in the fifth row, Tommy could see that something was different.

His father was an imposing figure when he stood in the pulpit. He spoke with a deep commanding voice. The congregation knew these things and responded with full attention. Today, they, too, saw more in their pastor, and with Tommy, waited silently.

Emotion and excitement flowed from Rev. Wilson as he began speaking.

"Today in Virginia a great battle is raging. Our brave men are fighting and dying for our cause. But they suffer greatly from lack of ammunition."

Rev. Wilson paused and looked earnestly into the faces of his parishioners. Then he startled them all as he continued.

"We . . . we here today, have the means to help our brave boys. We have the means to aid General Lee and his cause. We must do our duty. As soon as we are dismissed by the singing of the Doxology, we will all go directly to the Arsenal and help prepare the ammunition so badly needed by our boys."

He paused for only a brief second this time. Then with a great lifting of his arms, he bade his congregation rise. His commanding voice led the singing of the Doxology.

"Praise God from whom all blessings flow,
"Praise Him all creatures here below . . ."

Along with the congregation, Tommy sang the familiar words, but today they took on new meaning. They seemed to be a call-to-arms, a directive to action.

As soon as the brief song ended everyone quickly left the massive church. The parishioners, mostly women at this point in the war, headed up The Hill toward the Arsenal. A few quickly planned a lunch that could be prepared in various homes and taken to the Arsenal workers. Young and old, everyone wanted to help.

Especially Tommy. Feeling the same excitement as the other members of his father's church, Tommy rushed to him and asked what he could do. Much to his delight his father told him that he could, along with his friend Will Fleming, who was a year older than Tommy, take the family horse and carriage and collect the lunches being prepared by the women.

So the afternoon went. Well-dressed church-goers worked side-by-side with the regular ammunition laborers. Soon all were dirty and sweaty, but no one minded. By the end of the day, a railroad freight car was loaded with cartridges and the nine o'clock shipping deadline had been met.

Throughout all this, Tommy and Will made numerous trips back and forth across town and up The Hill. They picked up and delivered freshly prepared food, returned empty containers, waited while they were refilled, and then took more food up The Hill.

That Sunday young Tommy became an active participant in the war effort. The war was no longer just parades, the tolling of Big Steve, or news from afar. It was now action at home. Tommy felt the flush of excitement that comes with feeling that you are taking part in a great effort. He was to remember that Sunday for the rest of his life.

Chapter 8

A Decision is Made

One hot August day Tommy sat on the front steps waiting impatiently for his father. The town was quiet and sad. Black bows hung from many front doors in Augusta.

The Battle of Chickamauga was only a week past and each day more Augusta families learned of loved ones who were killed or wounded in that bloody battle on the "creek of death" in the North Georgia mountains. The Clinch Rifles alone had lost 194 men in the battle.

The mayor had called a meeting of important men in the city, and Rev. Wilson was one of them. All morning Tommy waited, curious about what the mayor might want with his father. Finally, seeing his father turn the corner, Tommy jumped up and ran to him.

"Father, what did he say? Why did he want to see you?"

Rev. Wilson placed an arm around the shoulder of his young son and continued walking. He said nothing.

"What did he say about the war? Was there a new battle? Tell me," Tommy demanded.

"Wait, wait. I need something cool to drink. While I get some water, you find your mother and sisters and meet me in my study. Then I'll tell all of you the news. It's going to affect us all."

Although anxious to hear the news, Tommy waited as patiently as possible for he knew his father would not be hurried. Finally all the family, and old Mittie and Samuel too, were gathered and his father was ready.

"As you know there has been a lot of fierce fighting lately and we have lost several battles and many men. Many more are wounded." Everyone in the room knew that he meant not just Augusta and Georgia, but the entire Confederacy.

"Chickamauga," he continued "is just the latest fierce and costly battle. Our wounded need help."

"Do you want our sewing circle to make more bandages?" Mrs Wilson asked before her husband could continue. She and the women of Augusta, like the women in all Southern towns, were busy making bandages and uniforms for the Confederate soldiers.

"We can help," Marion said. Annie showed her agreement by nodding her head.

"Wait, wait," Rev. Wilson interrupted. "While we will most certainly soon need more bandages, what is needed at the moment is more hospital space. The meeting today was to discuss the use of our churches as hospitals."

"Like at the Medical College?" Tommy asked, remembering the sights he had seen at the hospital there. It was only one block away, just past his father's church. From the churchyard he had seen the new buildings and the soldiers who had been sent there.

Looking from her husband to her son, Mrs. Wilson was not able to prevent a startled gasp from escaping from her throat.

"Oh, Joseph," she said turning back to him, "is it really going to happen. I want to help as much as possible, but in the church? Think of the blood and dirt and smell. Will it work?"

"It will have to work," her husband responded, "for the churches have been studied, and the Confederate surgeon says that no church is better suited for hospital use than the Presbyterian Church. It, along with several other churches, will be used as a hospital."

"Our church," whispered Tommy looking first at his mother and sisters and finally at his father. "Our church."

"Yes, our church," replied his father with a sigh.

Mrs. Wilson and the girls all begin to question Rev. Wilson at the same time. Tommy was talking excitedly to no one in particular. Only Mittie and Samuel remained quiet.

"Shh," Rev. Wilson said. His face was solemn. Everyone stopped talking and looked at him. After a brief silence, he continued.

"There's more," he said. "In addition to space for our wounded, space is needed for Union prisoners. We have also been given that honor. It seems that our churchyard is just the place for prisoners."

"Prisoners? Here?" Tommy asked in a loud voice.

Marion and Annie, too startled to speak, looked at each other in surprise and held tightly to one another's hand.

"Oh, Joseph, you can't mean it. Prisoners of war, in our own front yard," Mrs. Wilson cried.

"In our own churchyard, Mommy. In our own churchyard," young Tommy corrected her.

☆☆☆☆☆☆☆

Almost immediately after his father's meeting with the mayor, 220 patients arrived at the Presbyterian Church. An equal number went to St. Mary's Catholic Church located in the block west of Tommy's father's church and sitting directly across Telfair Street from the Manse and Tommy's bedroom windows. Scattered throughout Augusta at other hospital locations and in private homes were over 700 additional patients. And so the war, something real but distant, something at once glorious but not, again touched home.

Chapter 9

The Dead, the Dying, the Enemy

The future President of the United States stood on the edge of the field, fascinated by the parade passing by. He had seen many parades since the war began two years ago, but this one was different. There were no brass bands playing, no freshly uniformed infantry units stepping high, and no high prancing cavalry horses.

Neither the Oglethorpe Light Infantry, the Washington Artillery, nor the Clinch Rifles, a crackerjack unit of sharpshooters, were marching and filling everyone in their town with pride. In fact, no one was marching, and no one was cheering. There were no handkerchiefs and hats waving, and no one was whistling that snappy new tune, "Dixie's Land."

This was not a parade of clean, smartly dressed military men. This was a parade of ragged men in tattered uniforms. Their sabers and sashes replaced by blood and bandages. And dirt.

There was no one to watch this parade by the railroad tracks in Augusta, Georgia, but seven-year-old Tommy and his young friends. While playing in the fields by the railroad tracks, they heard the solemn ringing of the troop train's bell. They watched as it inched its way across the bridge over the Savannah River. The slow-moving train lumbered along the tracks until it finally shuddered to a stop beside the field. Curious, the boys ran to the train, and the parade began as wooden ramps were dropped from each car to the dry earth below.

Slowly the train emptied its cargo of Civil War wounded. A few limped unaided, but many more shuffled by, supported on one or both sides by others who were themselves wounded. Some hobbled on crutches, their legs bandaged. They kept their eyes downcast. One man, with a foot missing, kept his head down and his eyes on the bandage at the end of his leg. He seemed to be looking at the foot that wasn't there.

After the walking wounded parade, came men on litters. Their bodies, their heads, their limbs wrapped in bloody, dirty bandages. Some of the blood was old and caked; some new and oozing. The dirt came from the battlefield, the field hospital, and from the smoke-belching locomotive on the long train ride.

The litters were carried slowly by other dirty, grimy men. Tommy and his friends watched the procession and heard the soft, muffled moans of pain and human agony. The men on litters looked alike, yet different. Their faces were pale beneath the dirt. Their eyes were vacant, staring without seeing.

One man alone seemed to notice the presence of the boys. His large body was covered by a blood-soaked blanket on which several medals and many flies competed for space. His head and face were covered with bloody, dirty bandages. Only one eye was left uncovered. The eye stared blankly at the boys then down at the blanket-covered body. Finally it lifted back to the boys and as the litter moved past them, it swung sideways in its socket to hold them in its view for as long as possible. As the one-eyed, blanket-covered soldier passed, the boys could see that he was crying.

A foul, wretched smell filled the air through which the litters moved. It was not a smell like the barnyard or cowpen. It was not even a smell like the sickening odor of hogs being slaughtered and rendered into bacon and ham and chitterlings and lard. No, this smell was worse, much worse. As it grew stronger, Tommy and his friends covered their mouths and noses, as if to protect themselves from this smell which instinctively they knew to be the smell of death.

Finally, from the car nearest the engine came a different sight, men under guard. Men whose arms and legs were bound together, making it hard for them to walk. So, they, too, shuffled. And they, too, were covered with dirt and blood and bandages.

It seemed unreal, yet as young as the boys were, they knew that it was all too real. The loyal wounded and the enemy prisoners had arrived.

One of Tommy's friends broke their silence. "Come, on," he said. "Lets get back to our game."

Everyone turned to go but Tommy. Tommy stood still, only his head moving to follow the hundreds of wounded and dying soldiers who were passing by.

"Tommy, are you coming with us?" his friends asked.

Instead of answering, Tommy turned and headed back to his home and the security of his family. He could play no more today. He wasn't sure he could ever play that game again. The boys had been playing war.

Tommy's father's church, the First Presbyterian of Augusta, where Tommy observed both the Confederate wounded and the Yankee prisoners.

Chapter 10

A Place of Peace

As always, home did provide Tommy with comfort. Although he couldn't describe to his mother what he had seen, just being with her comforted him.

Finally he was able to ask, "Mother, why do you think our church was one of the ones chosen to be a hospital and prison yard?"

Mrs. Wilson had been arranging fresh flowers recently cut from her garden in the side yard. She stopped what she was doing and sat down next to her son.

"Some might say that our church was one of the churches chosen because of its size and grounds," she said, "but, I think the mayor and his committee felt the safety and peace that I always feel when I am in the church."

She paused for a moment and then asked Tommy, "Do you feel safe and peaceful when you are in the church?'

Without having to think, Tommy answered with a soft, "Yes. Yes, I do."

"Also," his mother continued, "our church is big enough to take care of many. Don't you agree?"

Tommy did, and, going to the front door, he looked across the street to the church. Gazing at the church he was satisfied with his mother's explanation for the First Presbyterian Church of Augusta, his father's church, was big and broad. Made of brick covered with stucco, the main building was surrounded by battlements and a centered square tower. Resting above all this was the steeple Tommy could see from his window.

Inside, the church was light and spacious. The dark wood of the pews, the massive altar and the wide aisles seemed to welcome all who entered. It looked solid and able to withstand anything asked of it, and soon it did. The pews were removed and replaced by cots and medical supplies. The perfect place for wounded men.

Surrounding all this were spacious grounds. Trees provided shade; a fenced yard provided confinement. The perfect place for Union prisoners.

Tommy knew that his father was at the church/hospital at that very moment. He was there doing whatever he could for the soldiers. Even before the wounded arrived, in fact, since early in the war, Rev. Wilson had been constantly involved in many acts of support for the Confederate troops.

He had made several trips to the front to offer spiritual support to the boys and to distribute Bibles. He had taken packages and letters to local troops stationed away from home. His longest time away from home and with the troops was for three months in the summer of 1863 when he reported for duty as Chaplain for the Confederate army.

Tommy looked back at his mother. He wondered if she would go to the church/hospital that day. If she did, she would probably care for some of the men he had seen getting off the train. For a long time she had been working with the Women's Society of the Presbyterian Church, a group of ladies who made bandages and garments needed by the soldiers.

Now, the location of the hospital in her husband's church provided her with the perfect opportunity to do more. As the wounded arrived, she helped care for them, preparing and changing dressings, and with the help of old Mittie, preparing food. Her maternal nature was free to give aid and comfort to those wounded housed within the family church.

And the numbers of wounded increased. After that first somber parade of wounded, Tommy and his friends watched as other ill and dying men slowly made their way on foot or on stretchers from dirt fields of the nearby Georgia Railroad Depot, down Walker Street to his father's church or to St. Mary's, or to the Augusta Medical College. They watched, too, as they came from the other direction, from boats on the Savannah River just five blocks away.

And so, while not witnessing the fighting, Augusta and Tommy witnessed the results of the fighting as the number of Confederate wounded continued to grow. Battered and bruised they came. Dead and dying they came. Legless, armless, eyeless, spiritless they came. The Confederates.

And so, too, came the Union soldiers. The prisoners. They were dirty, fearful men. Tommy gazed upon them in wonder. From his front steps he could see them. From his father's study he could see them. He could even see them from his window overlooking the church spire. They were the enemy. The Yankees.

From this window young Tommy could see his father's church and prisoners in the churchyard.

Chapter 11

Father's Study

Tommy stopped at the doorway to his father's study. He peeked in and saw Rev. Wilson on the floor.

"May I come in, father?" Tommy asked. But he did not wait for an answer, for he knew he was almost always welcome in his father's study which was a friendly place, a gathering place for the family.

It was big, broad, and almost square. It had two tall windows which looked out onto the front of the house and two windows which looked out onto the side yard and street. Between those two windows was a cozy fireplace that warmed the room in winter. From any of these windows, Tommy could see his father's church.

The room smelled of old books and tobacco. Rev. Wilson enjoyed smoking a clay bowl pipe when reading or working. His tobacco and pipes were kept in this, his room.

The room was lined with books. There were books about religion and Bibles, of course, but there were also novels such as those by James Fenimore Cooper, Charles Dickens, and Sir Walter Scott. Travel and poetry books could also be found on the numerous shelves.

These books were an important part of Tommy's life, but he didn't read them for himself. There was usually a family member ready to sit down and read to Tommy. If no one was available, Tommy would wait, often impatiently, for someone to read to him. When Tommy finally did read a book for himself, after the age of nine, it was in this familiar room where he found it. The book was Reverend Weems' *Life of George Washington*.

In this comfortable room, the family read together daily from the big leather Bible. In it Rev. Wilson penciled in notes and often read the scripture in the language of the day to make it more understandable for his children.

This room heard the family singing together, for Sunday evenings were family songfest time as they sung all their favorite hymns, unaccompanied by musical instruments. Also in this room, the family prayed together daily on bended knee. This was a practice that would stay with Tommy for the rest of his life.

Here, too, the family played games together. They played chess, at which Tommy wasn't very good, and word games which involved punning and deciphering meanings. Elsewhere in the house they played billiards, or pool. Tommy was better at billiards than at chess. Although card games were popular, Rev. Wilson did not allow them in his home. They were too much like gambling.

"Are you busy," Tommy asked, looking down at his father.

Tommy had lost his baby chubbiness. His thin hair floated across his high forehead. His eyes gazed intently, partly from interest in things and partly from poor eyesight. Those same eyes could stare coldly at someone when his temper was readily to flare.

"I'm not busy, son," Rev. Wilson replied to his son's question. "You know you're always welcome in here. Well, almost always," his father chuckled. "Flip over a chair and join me."

Smiling, Tommy took a straightback chair, turned it upside down on the floor, sat down, and leaned against the back of the chair. The family was never surprised to find Rev. Wilson on the floor like this, for it was one of his favorite reading positions.

"I like this room, "Tommy said to his father. "It is a lot like you."

"Oh, so you think I'm big, broad, and stuffy and smell like tobacco?" his father joked.

"Well, in a way," Tommy joined in the humor as he looked around the room.

Father and son were both quiet for a while. Finally, looking at the large windows through which the winter sunshine was pouring, Tommy decided to talk with his father about something that was on his mind.

"Father," he said solemnly, "I can see the prisoners in the churchyard from these windows. Do you think they can see us?"

"Well," replied Rev. Wilson thoughtfully, "I suppose they can, at least at night if the lamplight is just right." He looked closely at his son. "Why? Does that worry you?"

"Well, I'm not sure. I've watched them from this room and from your's and mother's bedroom and even from the nursery room." He paused and looked toward the window closest to the churchyard-turned-prisonyard. "I've often wondered if they were watching back."

"Now, Tommy," his father began, but before he could say more, Tommy interrupted him.

"They are Yankees, Father," he said seriously. "They might be spying on us."

For a moment his father didn't respond. Finally he said, "Yes, Tommy, they are Yankees, but they're also men. Men who are willing to fight for something they believe in. You have uncles who are Yankees, you know."

"I know," said Tommy remembering his divided family. The Wilsons and Woodrows were literally brother against brother. Rev. Wilson, born in Ohio to an abolitionist father, was nevertheless steadfast in his Southern sympathies. Some of his brothers were equally as loyal in their union sympathies. In fact, two of his brothers were generals in the Union army.

Tommy's mother's family was also divided in its loyalties. Her father, Tommy's Grandfather Woodrow who read the Bible in Greek and Hebrew on his way to breakfast and who sang old Scottish ballads while smoking a pipe and enjoying a toddy, was a Union sympathizer. Her sister and brother, now living in the South, were Confederate in their sympathies.

His father continued, "I don't imagine those men in the churchyard spend too much time looking at the windows of our house. Many of them are sick or wounded and their stay in our churchyard is usually short."

"I've often wondered. Where do they go when they leave here?" Tommy asked. "Are they still prisoners, or do we let them go back to fight against us again?"

"Oh, I'm sure the Confederacy doesn't want them fighting against us again. No, they go on to a more permanent war prison camp like Millen or Andersonville." Turning back to his son, he added, "I don't want you to worry too much about those men. Do you think you can promise that?"

"I'll try," promised Tommy, unsure that he could keep that promise, but willing to make the effort.

Rev. Wilson gave Tommy a smile, took a puff on his pipe and challenged Tommy to a game. "Good," he said. "Now, how about a game of billiards. Do you feel lucky today? Or would rather find someone to read to you?"

Chapter 12

Cowpea Soup and Plug Tobacco

"Cowpea soup, again," muttered Tommy as he sat down for dinner. The entire family had been waiting for him so that father might ask the blessing.

Everyone bowed their heads as Rev. Wilson began. "Our father, make us all eternally grateful for the food we are about to receive. We remember those who are less fortunate and ask that you bestow your blessings upon them. Amen."

"They can have my soup," Tommy said softly, but not so softly that his father did not hear.

"Now, Tommy, you may stay and eat what Mittie and your mother have worked so hard to provide for us, or you may go to your room." His father looked at him questioningly. "Well? Which shall it be?"

Tommy propped his feet up on his favorite spot under the table, hoping that his father wouldn't notice. He looked around the big bright dining room. His mother sat opposite his father at one end of the dark mahogany table. Marion and Annie sat across from him. In the center of the table was his mother's favorite fresh cut flowers arranged in an overflowing display. Large trays of cornbread sat on each side of the flowers. The everyday china and silver gleamed at each place. It was an inviting setting.

But cowpea soup again?

With men away from home in the armies, most local plantations were able to grow only enough food for their own families so the variety of food in town was limited. Small backyard gardens, such as Tommy's family had, could grow only small amounts of food.

But both backyard gardens and undermanned plantations could grow cowpeas. They grew abundantly and without much effort on anyone's part. Therefore, cowpeas were readily available when many other foods were not.

Tommy knew that cowpeas were forage food, food grown for the cattle to eat, not especially for people to eat. These cowpeas, or black-eyed peas as they would later be called, were, however, perfectly safe for people to eat. And many did.

Tommy looked around the table. His family was waiting for his reply. He looked behind the table at Mittie who was standing near the walkway to the kitchen waiting to serve the family.

"I'll stay," he said softly, hoping that would be the end of it, knowing it wouldn't.

"Say exactly what you mean, Tommy," said his father, not in anger but, as always when he wanted his son to speak clearly, with great patience.

"I will stay and eat dinner with the family," said Tommy, thinking that must be clear enough, but in case it wasn't, he added, "The soup will be fine, and the cornbread does smell delicious."

He looked from his father to his mother and then to old Mittie. All three nodded and smiled at him.

"Good," said Rev. Wilson. "Mittie, we can begin."

"Father, what did you buy while you were out?" asked Annie, glad that they could get on with the meal and any news her father might have.

"Are there any new books in town?" Marion asked, hoping there would be.

"Or newspapers?" added Mrs. Wilson.

"No new books or outside newspapers, nothing new. There is still very little to buy," he replied.

As the war years crept by, the South was cut off not only from food and but also from other supplies. War-shattered railroads stopped the movement of grain, vegetables, and meat. It stopped the movement of shoes, clothing, and toys. It stopped the movement of books and newspapers and many other items Southerners were used to getting.

Some goods were available for purchase at different times but were high in price and often low in quality. Soap might cost $25 a bar, a young boy's wool cap, $120, and everyday china cups, $125 each. Salt, once so plentiful and something most Southern cooks never dreamed of doing without, was selling for $35 a pound or $150 a bushel. By the end of the war, it was completely unavailable.

Rev. Wilson took a bite of cornbread and smiled up at Mittie. "The cornbread lives up to Tommy's expectations, Mittie. I don't know how you do it."

"Thank you, sir," Mittie replied, looking at Mrs. Wilson and smiling. "We manage, sir, we manage," she continued as she headed out the door.

"Oh Mittie," Rev. Wilson stopped her. "Please tell Samuel that I will need his help with the attic stairs after we finish. I have something to put up there."

☆☆☆☆☆☆

No one asked, for they all knew. What Rev. Wilson had to put in the attic was plug tobacco, something that he himself did not use, but something which was expected to become valuable as an item for barter. The numerous shortages meant that Southerners had to learn to make do and bartering, or trading one item for another, was fast becoming the way many got the goods they needed.

Even families who were considered fairly well off, like the Wilsons, felt the shortages. Now, they, too, ate cowpea soup, made toys from old broomsticks and discarded fabrics, and refashioned last year's clothing.

These shortages and high prices brought about a fear of what the future might hold. And so hoarding, or putting away items that might be valuable in the future, became a part of life for many Southerners. Plug tobacco became valuable and its value was expected to increase. Therefore, whenever he could buy it, Rev. Wilson did so and hid it in the attic.

Years later, when Tommy was Woodrow Wilson, twenty-eighth President of the United States, rationing, or limiting how much a person can buy, was initiated as part of the World War I relief effort. He remembered those Civil War days when his family had been forced to do without. It wasn't so bad, he insisted, and he remembered that his mother had made a "delicious" cowpea soup. Even if it was unsalted.

Chapter 13

Waiting for Sherman

"Well," said Will Fleming to his friends who were gathered in Tommy's backyard, "General Sherman has left Atlanta and he's headed for Augusta."

"We all know that," said Tommy. "I thought you said you had news for us." He looked around at the other boys who nodded in agreement.

"Yeah," said another of the boys, "we know Sherman burned Atlanta and wants to burn all of us as he marches across Georgia. Tell us something new."

"He'll be here in two days," said Will with authority.

"In two days?" someone asked.

"How do you know that, Will?" asked another.

"I just left Broad Street," Will continued, "General Fry has all his men putting in guns to use when Sherman gets here."

"Guns?" someone whispered.

"In town?" one of the boys asked, "that close?"

"Lets go see," someone suggested, and all the boys jumped up and headed for the heart of town just three blocks away.

Early in the war, the boys had been forced to stay within the gates of their homes, but now, like the war, they were older and could wander about town by themselves. Going downtown was a common experience for them.

They knew that cotton had been piled high waiting for Sherman, but guns were something new. They wanted to see for themselves.

Before reaching their destination, the frantic activity told them that Will was right. Trenches were being dug, earthwork fortifications were being built, and sandbags were being filled. Earthen forts would soon cover the entire downtown area.

"Wow," said one of the younger boys, at a loss for more words.

"Boys, you're gonna have to move on outta the way," a soldier yelled. "We got work to do here."

Tommy and Joe looked at each other and looked back to the soldier, a stranger. This was their town and they wanted to know what was going on.

"Exactly what are you doing?" asked Tommy with an air of authority.

Slightly amused, the soldier took a brief break. Leaning on his shovel, he told the boys what he knew.

"Well, now, eventually these here fortifications will cover a large quarter-moon shaped area. They will go all the way from the Savannah River," he nodded to his right, "to the Powder Works and railroad line out on The Hill." He nodded to his left. "Y'all know where I'm talking about, don't you?"

The boys nodded. Of course they knew. They all had friends and relatives who lived on The Hill, three miles outside of town.

"Well then, all along the way guns will be placed on the railroad lines," the soldier finished knowingly.

"Wow," several of the boys responded. They thought for a moment and looked at each other and wondered what was about to happen to them and their world.

"All right, move on now," their informer told them. "Move on, we've got work to do."

Tommy and his friends wandered up Broad Street away from the soldier. They stopped to look at the bales of cotton.

"Burn them all at once," one of the boys said, probably echoing discussions he had heard at home.

"Yes, and do it quickly," another said.

"But don't do it at night. Sherman might see the flames," added a third.

"Yes, but if he sees the flames, maybe he will think we've been attacked by another division of the Union Army and leave us alone," replied the first boy.

"Maybe we shouldn't burn it," one timid voice ventured.

"If we don't, he will," said another. "And who knows what else he might burn."

The object of all this discussion was cotton, numerous bales of cotton piled high just waiting for the people of Augusta to set fire to them before the enemy could. The boys didn't know it at the time, but Union General William Tecumseh Sherman would march a few miles west of Augusta, and the cotton would not be burned, either by local citizens or the enemy.

Chapter 14

The Season to be Jolly

"How are we going to celebrate Christmas this year?" Annie asked her mother.

"Just as we always do," replied Mrs. Wilson, "with love, and joy, and thanks."

"Yes, mother, but how about festivities, and decorations, and gifts?"

"It does seem like forever since we've had anything to celebrate," added Marion.

"And don't forget," chimed in Tommy, "someone important has a birthday just three days after Christmas."

Three sets of feminine eyes looked at Tommy, looked at each other, and rolled in unison.

"Oh, please," said Mrs. Wilson, "one thing at a time."

It was mid-December, 1864, and the Wilson family, along with all of Augusta, was still feeling enormous relief that Sherman's troops had recently taken a more direct route to Savannah and left them untouched. A feeling of celebration was in the air.

"Mother, you've never said anything about it, but why do you think Sherman passed us by?" asked Marion, doing as hundreds of Augustans did daily, speculating on Sherman's motives for sparing their city.

"I'm sure I don't know," replied Mrs. Wilson, not willing to be drawn into the game.

"I think it really was because he had met and fallen in love with an Augusta girl while her brother and Gen. Sherman were in military school together," said Annie, preferring the romantic explanation.

"Maybe he really did like the city when he was stationed here at the Arsenal," said Marion. "It is a nice town, and especially on The Hill where the Arsenal is located. I can't imagine anyone, even Sherman, wanting to burn that."

"I think he knew we were ready for him," said Tommy, remembering the elaborate fortifications. "He probably sent in a spy to look the town over and the spy told him we were ready and waiting for him. So he went another way."

"Children, children," said Mrs. Wilson. "I never thought I'd say this, but let's turn our thoughts and this conversation back to Christmas and how we should celebrate this year. We'll have to make do and improvise a lot, you know. Supplies are still short, and money scarce."

"And everything is priced high," said Tommy. When his mother and sisters looked at him in surprise, he smiled and said, "Well, that's what everyone says."

Chapter 15

It's Over

"I can't believe it's over," one of the boys said.

"Thank God it's over," said Tommy, echoing words he had heard at home.

"Yes," another said sadly.

"I never thought it would end," said another, "especially this way."

"I know, I thought we would win."

"Did you really?" someone asked in surprise.

"Well, yes, at first I did. And I always wanted to believe we would," came the reply.

"Yes, at first," several of the boys echoed.

The boys were in the hayloft of the small stable in Tommy's backyard. The door was closed and it was dark and stuffy inside. But they didn't mind, for the place seem to echo most of their feelings.

"But, I'm glad it's over," someone said timidly, as if the speaker expected strong opposition to his words.

"Me, too," came another voice.

"Me, too," came several echoes.

"Can you remember before the war?" someone asked.

"Not me."

"Not me."

"Do you realize that half our lives have been spent during this war?" a thoughtful voice said.

"It's all I remember," said another.

"I'm really glad it's finally over."

"Should we celebrate?" someone asked.

After a thoughtful silence, a reply came out of the darkness.

"Tomorrow."

It was over. The war that crossed five Aprils, from April 12, 1861, to April 9, 1865; the war that cost 600,000 lives; that cast brother against brother. The war that had many names: The Civil War, The War Between the States, The War for Southern Independence, The War Against Northern Aggression, Mr. Lincoln's War, and afterwards in the South, The Late Unpleasantness.

The war of hundreds of skirmishes and battles, fought in hundreds of places, was over. The war that in some way touched every place and every citizen of the South, including Augusta and the future Woodrow Wilson, was finally over. It was the war that years later, along with his father's teachings, led President Woodrow Wilson to strive for a lasting peace. And while that lasting peace was not to come, President Wilson, young Tommy, was to become only the second U.S. President to be awarded the Nobel Peace Prize.

Part 2:

RECONSTRUCTION YEARS

1865-1870

Chapter 16

The May Day Riots

Tommy was playing in his back yard with Joe and Phil. They were building forts under the large bushes. The forts were not war forts such as those they were now familiar with, but were, instead, forts which housed lords and ladies from Sir Walter Scott's adventures. Forts that had very little in common with everyday life in Augusta.

Mittie approached the boys and told Tommy that his mother and father wanted to see him inside. She looked at Joe and Phil.

"You two go on along home, now," she said. "I 'spects you goin' hear dis same thing at home." She helped dust the dirt from their clothing, "Yes, sir, our Rev. and your daddy been talking together a long time dis mornin'. I 'spects you going to hear dis, too."

The boys looked at each other and looked at Mittie.

"What, Mittie?" Tommy asked. "What? Does this have something to do with last night?"

"We know there was fighting last night, Mittie," added Joe. "We saw the cannon fire explosions over the city and heard the noise, but its quiet now," he finished.

"Do you know what's going on?" Phil asked the old servant.

"All I know," replied Mittie, "is that Master Tommy here needs to git on in the house and you two better run on home to your own folks. Scat now," she continued, waving her white apron as if it were a red flag and the boys charging bulls. "Scat, now."

Tommy followed Mittie into the house and joined his mother and sisters in his father's study. He started asking questions, but his mother only shook her head and "shushed" him.

Shortly Rev. Wilson entered the parlor, followed by Mittie and Samuel.

"As you know," he said without giving anyone time to question him, "things have been unsettled in Augusta for some time. Since we recently learned of the end of the war, things have only gotten worse. Yesterday mobs ran wild around town. Stores were looted and private and governmental supplies taken."

Tommy knew all about that. People had been running back and forth in front of his house with bags of goods on their backs or under their arms. Some were in wagons, some on horses, some on foot. The noise from Broad and Greene Streets, where most of the looting was taking place, was often deafening.

Tommy, Joe, and Phil had wanted to go to the center of town and investigate, but neither of their families would let them go. They had been allowed to watch the proceedings only from one yard or the other. They had seen several men fighting at the corner of

Greene and McIntosh. When gunfire was heard, their mothers called them back inside their homes and later let them play only in the safety of the adjoining back yards.

So far, father had told them nothing they didn't already know.

"Father," Tommy started. His father held up his hand and shook his head. Tommy forced himself to remain quiet.

Father took a deep breath and went on. "Last night a man was shot to death down by the river bridge. The stables were set on fire, and order, such as it was, was maintained throughout the night only by armed patrols."

He turned from his family and servants and walked to the window and looked toward his church. With his back still to the small group, he continued.

"Early today the Federal officer in charge of Augusta declared martial law."

Mrs. Wilson gasped and with her hand over her heart asked, "just what does that mean, Joseph?"

"Yes, father, what?" asked Marion.

"It means that the city has been divided into small sections and each section has a Federal officer in charge," he replied as he turned back to them.

"In charge of what?" Tommy wanted to know.

"In charge of us," his father replied. "Simply put, we are under house arrest. We are to remain indoors unless on approved business."

After several minutes of confused reaction, with everyone talking at once, Tommy got his father's attention.

"By indoors, father, do you really mean indoors, or . . . " He was interrupted by his father.

"By indoors, Tommy, I mean indoors. You are not to be on the porch or in the yard and certainly not in the streets."

He looked at the small group made up of his wife, children, and Negro servants.

"This order," he said solemnly," applies especially to women, children, and Negroes."

Tommy looked around at his family and their servants. They all seemed lost in their own thoughts. For once, Tommy, too, was silent as he wondered about the future of his town.

Physically Augusta had fared much better than most Southern cities during the war. The streets and nearby countryside had not become actual battlefields. The homes and factories had not been destroyed. The city had been passed, not once, but twice by that master of destruction General Sherman.

But Augusta was ravaged emotionally. Citizens had watched as whole men left and wounded or dead men returned. They had watched as war refugees of all types flooded the city. Shortages of men, goods, and food, made life difficult. Threats of battle and oppression weighed heavily upon Augustans.

After the war, roaming bands of outlaws, rioting groups of freed slaves, and looting mobs of civilians devastated Augusta. And then the Yankees came. And they took over.

And so, in early May, less than a month after Gen. Robert E. Lee had surrendered to Gen. Ulysses S. Grant, Federal troops issued martial law. Under this order they controlled everything within the city. The kinder ones tried to help the crushed Confederates. The unkind ones, and the local citizens thought these far outnumbered the kind ones, only added to the misery and oppression.

During all this chaos, parades were still frequent in Augusta. Parades of highstepping, cheering freed Negroes with nowhere to go. Parades of bold daylight looters with stolen goods. Parades of Union soldiers marching to "Yankee" songs.

Then, just when Augustans thought they were at their lowest ebb, came more devastating news. The federal government had issued a million dollar reward for the capture of a Confederate hero -- Jefferson Davis, now the President without a country.

Chapter 17

A Fallen Leader

The May day was warm and sunny, abundant with colorful spring flowers. It was a perfect day for a parade. And there was a parade; but for the people of Augusta, it was not a joyous occasion. And it was not their parade.

Horse drawn wagons and military ambulances, loaded with baggage and rumpled military prisoners passed slowly along Broad Street. They were not Yankee prisoners as before, coming to be confined in Augusta. These were Confederates on their way to Union prisons. They sat solemnly atop the baggage, surrounded by military guards, Union soldiers who seemed to take pride in marching their captives through a Southern town.

Tommy and his family, along with a few friends, watched the procession from a darkened room. It felt cold in spite of the spring warmth outside. The shades were drawn. Late afternoon sunlight filtered through only when someone peeked out.

"I see him. He's coming," someone said, with an intake of breath and a quiver in the voice. Eagerly everyone crowded by the windows while a dozen pairs of hands held the shade back just far enough to peek out.

"Yes, its him," said Rev. Wilson. "It's him."

Tommy stretched to see. Yes, it was him -- Jefferson Davis, former President of the Confederacy, now a military prisoner and a man without a country, for the Confederacy had fallen and the Federal government would not readmit him as a citizen, even if he had been willing to sign the oath being required of all former Confederate citizens.

In the somber parade outside, Jefferson Davis was the most prized prisoner and the most heavily guarded. He did not look around. He sat still and focused his eyes on the many spring flowers that bordered the Augusta roadside.

"Why must they have so many guards around him?" asked Tommy, although he thought he knew the answer. "He looks too tired to try to escape."

"Perhaps the soldiers are not worried about his trying to escape," said his father. "Perhaps they are worried about someone trying to rescue him."

Tommy considered this for a moment but he didn't think a rescue attempt was likely. Looking up at his father, he realized his father didn't think so either.

Again watching the slow procession, Tommy remembered the story of how Jefferson Davis, President of the Confederacy, had been captured beside a creek north of Irwinville, Georgia. His wife and children and several Confederate officers were with him. All were taken into custody and marched to Macon. It was mid-May 1865, and the war had been over for one month.

The Davis family was then taken by train from Macon to Augusta where they were now being paraded through the streets to the river where they would board a river tug. Already on board was Alexander Stephens, vice-president of the fallen Confederacy. From Augusta the group would go downriver to Savannah.

Tommy later learned that upon reaching Savannah the group was transferred to an oceangoing steamer and sailed up the eastern coastline to Hampton Roads, Virginia. At that point the small group was separated and the leaders and officers of the Confederacy sent to various prisons in the North. Jeff Davis was sent first to Fortress Monroe, then to more permanent quarters at Fort HcHenry, Maryland.

Throughout all their travels after capture, crowds gathered along the way to see the fallen President and his family. The crowds were divided in their support of the Davis'. The union troops loudly and rudely booed and jeered both the Confederate President and his family. Some Southerners who felt Jeff Davis had disgraced the South by being captured while supposedly dressed in womens clothing, booed him, while others braved the hostility of the conquering Yankees and openly cheered Jefferson Davis and his family.

Still others, like the Wilsons and their friends, were unsure of the reaction they should have. They respected Jefferson Davis and the Southern causes. They knew, however, that too much public support might bring down the wrath of the Federal soldiers upon the city.

It was early evening, almost dark, when the captured Confederate President made his journey through Augusta. The Wilsons, like many, watched from the shelter of darkened rooms, the act in itself a sign of respect and a sign of the times.

Chapter 18

Converting Yankees into Presbyterians

"You shouldn't be so friendly with those men," Tommy's Aunt Marion said as he and cousin Jessie reached the front porch of Aunt Marion's house after yet another trip to the guard house next door.

"Oh, mother, they're very nice to us."

"And they're all very friendly," added Tommy, looking back across to the guard house. He and Jessie had been going there for months. It had become an added treat to the many already surrounding any visit to his Aunt and Uncle's home on The Hill.

"Do you know who they are?" Aunt Marion asked.

"Well, of course," came the response, "they're guards."

"And what are they guarding?" Aunt Marion continued.

"Well, us and The Hill, and the Arsenal, I suppose." Tommy replied. "Why, Aunt Marion?"

"Children, children. Your new friends are, indeed, guarding the Arsenal. The Yankees took control of it after the war."

"Mother, what are you trying to say?" asked Jessie.

"Just this. Your new friends fought against us during the war. They're Yankees, and I really don't think you should spend so much time at the guard house."

"Yankees?" exclaimed a startled Tommy.

"Yankees?" echoed Jessie.

The cousins looked at each other and remained quiet for a while, thinking over the startling news.

Tommy was well aware that Yankees were to be found throughout the town, but perhaps he never expected them to range out to The Hill, a place which had always represented happiness and freedom to him. The Hill was only a few miles from town and was not specifically one hill. It was an area 300 feet higher in elevation than the city itself. It was cooler than the city, and it had fewer mosquitoes.

Many people who had homes in the city built large rambling homes on The Hill. They, along with their families and friends, would escape to these cooler homes during the hot, humid Augusta summers. Tommy's Aunt Marion and Uncle James Bones, Jessie's parents, had a home on The Hill.

The Bones' home was next to the Arsenal, the same Arsenal seized from Federal troops before the war started. The same Arsenal used by the Confederates during the war. The same one now back in Federal control. Tommy and Jessie enjoyed watching the guards and visiting with them, never suspecting that they were Yankees.

Finally Tommy broke the silence.

"We've got to help them," he said solemnly to Jessie.

"Help who?" she asked.

"The Yankees," said Tommy.

"How?" came a confused reply.

Tommy and Jessie talked over various ways to help the Yankees. Finally, these two children whose lives were so tightly woven around the church admitted what they had known all along. There was only one answer.

"We have to change them, convert them into Presbyterians," Tommy finally said. "Then they won't be Yankees, they'll be good."

Chapter 19

The Family Grows

"Tommy, wake up," whispered his sister Marion. "He's here!"

"Who's here?" Tommy asked sleepily.

"Our little brother, that's who," exclaimed Annie. "Hurry, get dressed for breakfast. After we eat we can see him. So come on, we're waiting on you.

"Okay, get out, I'm on my way." he replied.

After the girls left the room, Tommy walked over to his back window and looked out. It was still very early morning and not much was going on in the backyard below. Mittie was quickly making her way into the house from the storeroom, but that was all the movement he saw.

When the family first moved into the new manse, Tommy had been given the nursery which adjoined his parents bedroom. It was from that room that he could see the church spire and hear the organist practicing.

Now his bedroom was across the hall from the nursery, a big sunny room which caught the morning sunlight through its big windows. The side windows of his new room looked out toward his friend Joe Lamar's house. The back windows looked out on the backyard below. He liked this room; it was a young man's room, not a baby's room.

Tommy was now ten and a half. He had been the baby until today, but he was growing up and didn't mind giving up his title to a little brother.

"Hey, he called softly to anyone who was listening. "What's his name?"

His name was Joseph Ruggles Wilson, Jr., and he was born on July 20, 1867. Called Josie, he was to be the last sibling. The family was now complete -- two boys and two girls, with a devoted set of parents. When Josie was born, Marion was almost seventeen and Annie was just two months shy of fourteen.

On that hot summer day when Josie was born, no one in the family could have imagined what the future might bring. No one was thinking of the girls and the marriages and families that waited in their futures. No one was thinking of the baby's future as an insurance executive. And no one could possibly have imagined that Tommy would not only become president of Princeton University, but also governor of New Jersey and President of the United States.

On that summer morning their only thoughts were on the new baby . . . another person within the family's circle of love.

Chapter 20

Childhood Friends

"I killed her, I killed her," Tommy yelled as he ran toward the house.

He and his mother and sisters were visiting his Aunt Marion Bones at her home on The Hill. Cousin Jessie, although younger than Tommy, was one of Tommy's favorite playmates.

Jessie was a tomboy. She and Tommy often read James Fenimore Cooper's Indian stories. They would then use wild berries to stain their skins, fashion Indian headdresses out of chicken feathers, and make tomahawks from tree branches so that they could become Indians.

Then quietly they would hide in the woods, and watch for other children in the area. Finally, with tomahawks held high above their heads and war-whoops filling the air, they would spring on their unsuspecting victims. It was all in good fun and everyone involved enjoyed the make-believe.

One day Tommy and Jessie's fantasy play became all too real. That day they were not Indians stalking victims, but Tommy, with bow and arrow, was a great white hunter. Jessie, always eager to please her favorite cousin, climbed a tree and pretended to be a squirrel. The great white hunter, using a real bow and arrow, sighted the squirrel down the shaft of his arrow and fired.

Jessie gasped and fell to the ground. When Tommy reached her, she was unconscious.

"Jessie, Jessie," Tommy cried. "Wake up. Get up."

When Jessie did not move, Tommy struggled until he had her in his arms, and then as quickly as possible carried her to the house. As he approached he shouted his distress and his guilt.

"I killed her, I killed her. It's no accident. I'm a murderer."

Jessie wasn't dead, of course. She wasn't even seriously injured, but that didn't erase the guilt Tommy felt for hurting one of his dearest playmates.

As he grew older, Tommy would spend less time with cousin Jessie. His playmates became the young boys in his neighborhood and later in his class at Professor Joseph Tyrone Derry's school. The "gang" included his next door neighbors Joe and Phil Lamar, Will Fleming, Tommy's assistant in the Sunday ammunition excursion, Pleasant Stovall, Tom Gibson, and Bill Keener.

The boys formed a club, the Lightfoot Baseball Club, partly a baseball club, partly a debating society. Tommy played second base for the club, but he was not one of the better players.

He was, however, the best speaker in the group. His father had tutored him for years to speak clearly and concisely. "Say what you mean," his father would direct him when he was struggling to make himself understood. The club offered Tommy the presidency and a chance to show his leadership.

Tommy remembered the meetings of the Presbyterian ministers who had gathered at his father's church early in the war. He remembered watching the moderator and the power he had as he controlled the group. The president of the Lightfoot Baseball Club could have this same power, Tommy thought, so he took his club presidency very seriously.

He demanded that the boys follow parliamentary procedure at all times. They could not speak until they were recognized by the president, Tommy. This gave him power and he used it. He would take his time calling on others to speak, and he would speak long and carefully about anything he felt like discussing.

He demanded that they stick to the procedure. When someone tried to interrupt him, they could see Tommy's displeasure as he looked at them over the rims of his eye glasses. They might feel the effects of his temper for he was headstrong and could totally ignore them if he chose to do so.

Tommy's speaking ability and delight in taking control of the situation were not the only reasons the boys elected him president of the Lightfoot Club. Quite simply, the best place around for holding club meetings was in the hayloft of the brick stable in Tommy's backyard. It was dark and cool inside. It smelled of horses, hay, and age.

Beneath a picture titled "His Satanic Majesty" the boys, more than one a preacher's son, would meet. "His Satanic Majesty," showing a devil, was an advertisement for deviled ham. All of this combined to make the hayloft just the place for a group of twelve and thirteen-year-old boys to meet and get away from the adults in their world.

When they were not holding club meetings, the boys would play hide-and-seek around town, catch rides on the streetcars, play ball, watch rooster fights, or simply sit in the shade of Big Steve or on the banks of the Savannah river and talk about life. Often those who lived in town would ride horses up The Hill or out into the nearby countryside to Westover, the Fleming family's plantation, and spend the day there with Will.

Whatever they did, Tommy joined in. And everything Tommy did, he did with enthusiasm; everything, that is, except study.

Chapter 21

The Reluctant Scholar

"Thomas Woodrow Wilson where have you been?" asked Professor Derry as he glowered at the young man.

Tommy glanced around the room for support. He had not been the only student skipping school that day. His friends did not look at him, and of course, no one answered.

"I've been to join the circus, sir," came the respectful reply.

"Join the circus?" Professor Derry asked in disbelief.

"Yes," replied Tommy. Again he paused, but there was still complete silence. "But I came back, you see, when I gave the matter more thought."

During the war years when Tommy's schoolhouse was the town of Augusta and when he was being educated by his father and mother, he had been a bright, eager student. He had loved learning, but his love for learning suddenly changed when Professor Derry, a Confederate officer, returned to Augusta after the war and opened an academy for boys just five blocks from the Wilson home.

Rev. and Mrs. Wilson looked over the school and its classes of Latin, history, writing, and bookkeeping. They decided that it was time for Tommy to go to school. It was 1866 when Tommy began his formal schooling. He was nine years old, and at that time he could neither read nor write.

Mr. Derry was very disappointed in young Tommy Wilson. Tommy spoke well, was a fountain of information, and a polite young man, yet he was lazy in his studies, disinterested in class, and likely to spend his time doodling. Drawing a baseball diamond and listing the names and positions of the players on the Lightfoot Baseball Team held more interest for Tommy than did his studies.

Until he was eleven or twelve, he was a poor reader and his marks were always below average. Modern educators have attributed Tommy's reading and attention problems to developmental dyslexia. But of course, Tommy's teacher had no such label to put on his student's apparent lack of interest and ability.

While the other boys in school may not have loved being in the classroom, they were, nevertheless, more attentive than Tommy. Professor Derry might not have been surprised years later when some of those boys achieved notable success. Joe Lamar would become an Associate Supreme Court Justice. Pleasant Stovall became a journalist and Minister to Switzerland. Bill Keener became Dean of the Law School at Columbia University, and Will Fleming became a lawyer and Georgia congressman.

But on the day the circus came to town, they were all drawn to it. And they were all caught.

"So you decided to come back to school?" Professor Derry asked.

"Yes, sir," replied Tommy, standing perfectly still.

He did not want to antagonize the teacher any more than he had already. And, he did not want the padding he had stuffed into his pants to shift. He knew that if Professor Derry chose to administer punishment he would need that padding in place.

As it turned out, the padding was needed.

Professor Derry administered the necessary punishment to his students, including Tommy. Perhaps if he had known in those early years that Tommy Wilson would someday be President of Princeton University and Governor of New Jersey, or that someday he would visit that disinterested student when he was President of the United States, Professor Derry might have been a happier man. But those days were far in the future and no one could have foreseen the road that lay ahead for the reluctant classroom student.

Chapter 22

The Hero

The Lightfoot Baseball Club members were sprawled in the shade of Big Steve. They had been practicing for their next game, but they were having a hard time keeping their mind on baseball. They, like all of Augusta, were still talking about their recent visitor, a revered leader, a hero in the finest sense of the word. Especially to Southerners in 1870, only five years after the end of the war.

"I can't believe he stayed here three days," said one of the boys for about the hundredth time.

"Well, he had to rest. This trip is to help improve his health, you know," said Joe knowingly.

"Is he really sick, do you think?" someone asked.

"Maybe not sick, just tired. His daughter is with him."

"Is she a nurse?" someone asked.

"No, I don't think so. She's just along to keep him company. She could take care of him, I suppose, if he needed her to," added Pleasant.

"I wish I had seen him," another said, again, not for the first time.

"Thank goodness he wasn't sent to prison like Jeff Davis," said Phil, with great feeling.

"You can't send a hero to prison. Even the Yankees know that. And they wanted him to lead their troops, too. They know how good he is. Or was."

"If he had led the Union Army, maybe the war would have ended sooner," someone said wistfully.

"He wouldn't do that. He's a Southerner," another exclaimed heatedly.

"He's an American. Even he says so."

"Well, whatever he is, he came to Augusta and I'm glad," said Joe.

Tommy had been unusually quiet during this discussion. He had heard it all before. He, like his friends, was still reliving the visit, and he knew they would soon get to him.

"It's too bad he didn't bring Traveller. I would love to see that horse. Do you think he still has him?" someone asked.

"Of course he still has him. I heard that the General rides him every day. He certainly wouldn't get rid of him. He must be about the best horse in the world. Imagine, going through all those battles without getting shot," replied Will, himself the owner of a fine horse.

The boys were silent for a moment. Each, perhaps, thinking how wonderful it would be to have a horse like Traveller, the most famous horse of the Civil War.

"I saw his carriage pass. He raised his hat in salute to all the old soldiers lining the street to honor him," one of the boys continued. "But I couldn't get any closer. Tell me again, Tommy, how you got so close to him."

Tommy smiled. He was thrilled that he had gotten close to their hero. He was even a little proud of the maneuvers that it took to get that near.

"Well, I pushed and shoved, and wiggled my way through a crowd. I knew he was up front somewhere. Why else would such a crowd be near the hotel and cheering so loudly?" Tommy paused to be sure everyone was listening to this retelling of his triumph.

"I was nice about it, of course." At this point his friends rolled their eyes and looked at each other. They knew how nice and forceful Tommy could be.

Tommy saw their looks, but he continued. "Soon I made my way to the front of the crowd. And there he was, right beside me!"

"Wow," came a chorus from his jealous friends.

"What did he say?"

"How did he look?"

"I'm not sure what he said. I was so excited that I don't remember if he said anything. Maybe he was just nodding and being polite. I really can't say." Tommy paused and thought about the meeting for the dozenth time during the past two days. He couldn't remember any words, just impressions.

"He looked dignified and brave. And bold. His hair was gray and so was his beard. He looked like a hero should look. He reminded me of the drawings of the Greek and Roman heroes that Professor Derry made us study."

"Were you really next to him? I mean, right next to him with no one between you?" asked an unbelieving friend.

"I was really right next to him. There was no one between us. He was tall and I had to look up to him. I guess I just stared up at him. I was too excited to even attempt to speak to him. But I was there, standing next to him. He looked at me and smiled."

The man Tommy and his friends and the rest of the town were still talking about was General Robert E. Lee, commanding officer of the Army of Virginia. A West Point graduate, he was acknowledged by both Confederate and Union alike to be a master military leader.

The last leader of the fallen Confederacy who had passed through Augusta had been Jefferson Davis. He had passed through in shackles, a symbol of the lost cause.

General Lee had come, not in shame, but as a reminder of the glory and honor of that lost cause. Even in defeat and surrender he had held his head high and represented his fallen South with dignity and grace. After the surrender, Lee stated that although he fought against the North, he did not hate it or its people and he reaffirmed his allegiance to the United States.

Even with his reaffirmation of loyalty to the Union as a whole, the U.S. congress refused to pardon Robert E. Lee or restore his citizenship. Still, he harbored no grievance or hatred. Through his strength and dignity, he showed a bruised and battered South how to act through difficult times.

And so, he came to Augusta, and Tommy was there. He did, indeed, push and wiggle his way to the side of Gen. Lee and looked up into the face of his hero. Almost thirty years later, while honoring Gen. Lee's memory on the 100th anniversary of his birth, Woodrow Wilson still remembered that day and called it a treasured memory of his childhood.

By the end of the year, the hero was dead.

By the end of that same year, Tommy no longer lived in Augusta.

Picture of loft above Wilson family's horse stables where Tommy and the Lightfoot Baseball Club met.

Chapter 23

Leaving Augusta

Tommy waited until all the members of the Lightfoot Club were seated and quiet. The members settled down quickly because their president looked very serious today.

"This meeting of the Lightfoot Club will now come to order," he said as he banged his gavel.

"Mr. Secretary, will you read the minutes of our last meeting." Everyone sat quietly as this was done. "Are there any amendments to the minutes?" There were none.

"Tommy, what's this all about? Why did you ask us to meet you here this morning?" asked Will.

"Chair has not recognized you, Will. You're out of order."

Will raised his hand. Tommy recognized him. "Mr. President, I move that we dispense with the reading of the treasurer's report since we don't really have any treasury to report and that we move on to the reason for this meeting."

"I second," said Phil Lamar.

"Its been moved and seconded . . ."

A chorus of "aye's" interrupted Tommy. When he did not remind the entire group that it was out of order, they knew something important was on his mind.

He continued. "Is there any old business?" Silence greeted his question.

Tommy took a long time and looked around the hayloft at his friends. The door was open and the early morning summer sunlight poured into the meeting area. His friends all looked at Tommy expectantly. He suddenly realized that this was going to be harder than he had thought.

Finally he became the club president again as he asked, "Is there any new business?" No one said anything. They just looked at Tommy and waited, almost forcing him to get on to the reason for this meeting.

"I have some new business," he said. "I'm afraid that I have to resign, not only as president of the Lightfoot Club, but as a member of the club also."

The last part of his statement was lost in the confusion of all the boys talking at once, asking why?

"Order, Order," demanded the president. He knew now it would be easier as long as the boys behaved in the orderly fashion of a regular club meeting.

The boys knew Tommy, and they knew that he would not continue until they sat down and got quiet. Looking at each other, asking questions with their eyes, they slowly settled down.

"Thank you," said Tommy. He paused again, adjusted the thin spectacles on his face and continued.

"My father has been offered a professorship at the Theological Seminary in Columbia, South Carolina," he said, removing his glasses and slowly cleaning them with his handkerchief. He put them back on his nose and continued. "My family is leaving Augusta. We're moving to South Carolina."

This time no amount of gavel pounding would bring order back to the hayloft. Tommy knew it, and suddenly he didn't want order.

He had stated his news as club president in an orderly fashion. Now he realized that he just wanted to talk about it with his friends. They were surprised and upset. They didn't want him to go. It felt good knowing that.

Epilogue

In the fall of 1870, three months before his fourteenth birthday, Tommy and his family left Augusta, a city that had been his home for almost thirteen years. There he had learned to walk and talk and play and share. There he had learned to read and write and think and lead. There, too, he had learned about God and the importance of family.

During those thirteen Augusta years, Tommy Wilson built his earliest memories. He made lifelong friendships, formed ideas that would stay with him forever, and experienced history that would shape the history he was later to help fashion.

After leaving Augusta, Tommy would spend five more years in the South. In later years, many would think of Thomas Woodrow Wilson as the President from New Jersey, but from his earliest experiences and in his own heart, he was a Southerner.

Although at the age of eighteen Tommy left the South to attend Princeton University and to begin the long road that would lead to his great successes, he would from time to time return and strengthen his Southern ties. After graduating from Princeton in 1879, he studied law at the University of Virginia in Charlottesville. While there, he made a decision that signified the end of his childhood. He changed his name.

"No one," he said, "can take seriously a man named Tommy." He immediately began signing everything Woodrow Wilson, and Tommy came to forever represent the past, his boyhood.

In May 1882 he moved back to Georgia and opened his first law office in Atlanta. Although he kept this office for only one year, it was an eventful year. During that year he met his future bride, Ellen Louise Axson of Rome, Georgia.

Born in Savannah, Georgia, Ellen was also the child of a Presbyterian minister. She was baptized at the Presbyterian Church at Beech Island, just outside Augusta, shortly after her birth. The Wilson family was present at that baptism and there is a family story that young Tommy held little Ellen at that time. He did not see her again until his return to Georgia as a young lawyer. Then, after a two-and-a-half year's courtship, they were married on June 24, 1885.

In 1902 Thomas Woodrow Wilson became President of Princeton University. Nine years later, in 1911, he became Governor of New Jersey. The following year he was nominated by the Democratic party as their candidate for President of the United States. He was elected to that office on November 5, 1912.

He was given the news of his election by his wife Ellen. Soon Woodrow, Ellen, and their three daughters moved into the White House. It was there that Ellen Axson Wilson died on August 6, 1914, after twenty-nine years of marriage.

President Wilson remarried in December 1915. The second Mrs. Wilson, Edith Bolling Galt of Virginia, lived until 1961. She had outlived her husband, the President, by thirty-seven years.

In 1924 Woodrow Wilson became ill. When news of his grave illness spread, a somber parade of grieving Americans kept watch and prayed outside his Washington, D.C. home. Finally word came. Thomas Woodrow Wilson, twenty-eighth President of the United States, was dead at the age of sixty-eight. Survived by his three daughters and his second wife, he was buried at the National Cathedral in Washington.

As an adult, Woodrow Wilson returned to Augusta only once. It was 1911 and he was governor of New Jersey with a major decision to make. Should he give up his governor's seat to run for President? He needed time to think as well as time to rest, and so he chose to return to the city of his childhood. In November he spent three days in Augusta. While there he walked the streets and toured the neighborhood he had known as a child.

On Sunday he attended his father's former church and afterward had lunch at the Manse. During lunch he recognized the dining room table as the one his family had used and even pointed out to the current pastor and his family marks that he had left under the table because of his habit of propping up his feet while eating. After lunch, he visited The Hill, that section of town which housed the Arsenal and where he had often visited his Aunt and Uncle and played with cousin Jessie.

During his stay in Augusta, he also went to a play to watch Ty Cobb, the baseball great, star in a local production of "The College Widow." After the performance, Woodrow Wilson was asked to make a short speech to the audience. He told the citizens of Augusta that he was enjoying his visit and enjoying remembering his childhood, reminiscing about the toddler who became a teenager as he lived and learned and worked and played for thirteen historic years in Augusta.

According to the local papers he said, "I am not thinking of myself as a man, but as a boy . . . And, tonight, I don't wish to be disturbed from my thoughts of my boyhood." So, for one more evening, Woodrow Wilson was Tommy.

Bibliography

GENERAL LIST:

Angle, Paul M., *A Pictorial History of The Civil War Years*. Garden City, N.Y.: Doubleday and Company, 1967.

Baker, Ray Stannard, *Woodrow Wilson, Life and Letters*. New York: Doubleday and Company, 1927-1939. 8 vols.

Blum, John Morton, *Woodrow Wilson and the Politics of Morality*. Boston: Little, Brown and Company, 1956.

Davis, William C, *The Battlefields of the Civil War*. London, England: Salamander Books Ltd., 1991.

Foote, Shelby, *The Civil War, A Narrative, Red River to Appomattox*. New York: Vintage Books, 1986.

Gragg, Rod, *The Illustrated Confederate Reader*. New York: Harper & Row, 1989.

Link, Arthur S, *Woodrow Wilson, A Brief Biography*. World Publishing. 1963.

Walworth, Arthur, *Woodrow Wilson*. Baltimore: Penguin Books, Inc., 1958.

SPECIAL LIST:

Askins, Norman Davenport, *Research Study: The Boyhood Home of President Woodrow Wilson, Augusta, Georgia for Historic Augusta, Inc.* Atlanta, 1994.

Corley, Florence Fleming, *Confederate City*. Columbia, 1960.

Thomas, Ella Gertrude Clanton, *The Secret Eye: The Journal of Ella Gertrude Clanton Thomas 1848-1889*, edited by *Virginia Ingraham Burr*. Chapel Hill. The University of North Carolina Press, 1990.

OTHER

Montgomery, Erick D., Executive Director, Historic Augusta. Oral history and private tour of the Woodrow Wilson Boyhood Home, Augusta, Ga., 1995.

Richland County Historic Preservation Commission. Oral history and private tour of the Woodrow Wilson Boyhood Home, Columbia, South Carolina, 1995.

Woodrow Wilson Birthplace and Museum. Oral history and tour. Staunton, Virginia 1996.

The Boyhood Homes of President Thomas Woodrow Wilson

The Woodrow Wilson Birthplace & Museum is located at 18-24 North Coalter Street, Staunton, VA, 24401. Open daily 9 to 5, March through November; and 10 to 4, December through February. There is an admission fee which includes both the birthplace home and the museum.

The Boyhood Home of President Woodrow Wilson is located at 419 Seventh Street, Augusta, GA. This home is not now open to the public for restoration is not complete. Restoration is a project of Historic Augusta, Inc., 10th Street, Augusta, GA.

The Woodrow Wilson Boyhood Home is located at 1705 Hampton Street, Columbia, S.C. It is open to the public Tuesday through Saturday. Tickets for tours and information may be obtained from Historic Columbia Foundation, 1601 Richland Street, 29201.

About the author . . .

Julia Faye Smith

Julia Faye Dockery Smith is a native of Alabama. She attended and graduated from local public schools in Tuscaloosa. She completed her undergraduate degree at the University of Montevallo, receiving a degree in education, with a major in English.

For several years, she taught special education and English in Florida high schools. After marriage to a journalist and several years' hiatus to raise three children, she returned to the classroom in Colorado, teaching English and reading at the middle school level. In 1982, she received her master's degree in reading from Colorado State University.

She has spent the past 15 years in middle school education, as a teacher and team leader and working on special projects. She developed middle school novel reading programs in both Colorado and Florida. While in Colorado, she was a district coordinator for the development of middle school Interdisciplinary Units. She now teaches middle school reading and social studies in Georgia.

She has written several novels, short stories, and picture books, mostly for the enjoyment of her family and friends, who have encouraged her to make the works more widely available.

Tommy, The Civil War Childhood of a President, is the result of Mrs. Smith happening, by chance, upon the Augusta, Ga., Boyhood Home of President Woodrow Wilson. She wanted to read of his Civil War childhood and when she searched for books on the subject, found there were none. She felt that the 13 years President Wilson spent in Augusta represented a singular moment in our nation's history and the most formative years of a young boy's life. Working from bits and pieces of information, searching records and journals of the time, and meeting with persons who are knowledgeable about his past, Mrs. Smith was able to write about President Wilson's youth. By then, she no longer thought of him as President Woodrow Wilson, but, like his family, she knew him as Tommy.